the little book of
crisis

The Little Book of Crisis: How to Cope with Change
© Frances Lincoln Limited 1999

Text copyright © Sally-Ann Lipson
Jacket design by Liz Lewis © Frances Lincoln Limited 1999

First published in Great Britain in 1999 by
Frances Lincoln Limited, 4 Torriano Mews, Torriano Avenue,
London NW5 2RZ

British Library Cataloguing in Publication Data
available on request

ISBN 0-7112-1558-8

Set in Spectrum and Frutiger

Printed in Hong Kong

9 8 7 6 5 4 3 2 1

the little book of ■ ■

crisis

HOW TO COPE WITH CHANGE

Sally-Ann Lipson

FRANCES LINCOLN

Introduction

Sooner or later there comes a time in life when we find ourselves at a crossroads, with no map or signpost and no landmark in sight to show where we're heading. We feel lost, uncertain, anxious, out of control. Life has changed, and that frightens us.

Change frightens us because we rely on familiar things and people to give us a sense of continuity. As long as they're there, we feel secure and safe. So when change comes along, we tend to act like ostriches and try to protect ourselves from change by ignoring it.

The truth is that nothing stays the same for ever. Everything changes: our bodies, what we believe, the way we feel about ourselves and others. Change is the only constant in the universe. We may dread it, but how can we learn to cope with it?

Crisis has many different stages. Each is a natural part of the process. People move through them at a pace and in a way that is right for them. Whatever stage you're in, it won't last for ever.

As you read this book, I hope you'll see that your crisis could be the most important thing to happen to you. In my own experience, every crisis has a gift to offer. The question to ask yourself is: am I ready to accept it?

The gift each crisis offers is unique. No one can predict in advance what it will be, or force it to be one thing rather than another. Perhaps the gift could be deeper understanding of yourself and others? Greater independence? New friendships? Keep an open mind and wait to find out.

Crisis gives us the chance to grow.

The gift is there for the taking.

Change

These are just a few of the changes
that can throw us into crisis.

illness

having
a baby

an accident

a crime

losing
a job

changing
jobs

the death
of someone we
care about

Some of these are what we might call a change for the better, but that doesn't mean they can't bring about a crisis.

Recognizing

Whatever the crisis is, at some point we recognize that

life has

changed

If you have already done this, congratulate yourself.
Once you recognize you're in crisis,
you can begin to do something about it.

The crisis within

Changes in the world outside are only part of the picture.
Crisis is about our inner world too:

beliefs

I can cope with anything.

I don't believe in asking for help.

attitudes

I'd never get a divorce.

Money's not that important to me.

feelings

I feel loved.

I feel safe living here.

and expectations

I'll work till I'm 65.

My parents will always be there.

Shattered

Change can smash your belief system to pieces.
When that happens, you may find yourself feeling:

desperate

anxious

crazy

unprotected

threatened

frightened

lost

But there's a positive side to crisis too.

When old beliefs are shattered we get room to change and grow.

Crisis can get us moving in a new direction.
It can make us pay attention to things
we'd rather ignore.

Look back over your life and ask yourself
when you learned the most.
The chances are it was when things went wrong,
when times were tough.
We don't learn much in the good times.

Transformation

Crisis can give us the energy to make the changes
we need to transform our lives.
What might be trying to emerge from your crisis?

patience
compassion
courage
wisdom

What quality could it be?

confidence
beauty
enthusiasm
serenity

Don't worry if you don't get an answer straight away.

creativity

hope

forgiveness

energy

It may take time before you know.

joy

understanding

strength

love

5 stages of change

A crisis is a process of intense change that goes on until it reaches its natural ending. The next pages are about the five stages people go through.

1 DENIAL

2 ANGER

3 BARGAINING

You can't tell how long a stage will last for you or what order they'll happen in. You may hop about from one stage to another, or find yourself in more than one stage at a time. There's nothing strange or wrong about that.

ACCEPTANCE

5

4

SADNESS & DEPRESSION

Wherever you are is where you need to be.

1

DENIAL

Leave me alone.

I'm perfectly all right.

It's all a mistake.

When you're in denial, you can't take in
what's happened.

You don't want to think or talk about it.

You may not even feel much at all.

After the shock of crisis,
denial and numbness can be a blessing.
They let you come to terms with change
gradually, in your own time.

2

ANGER

No one treats me like that!

I'll never forgive him.

It isn't fair.

You don't understand what it's like.

It's all her fault.

When you begin to take in what's happened,
numbness may give way to deep anger.

Wherever you look you find something to be
angry about.

Nothing is right.

It's easy to blame people in this stage.

Feeling angry is natural and healthy.
There are ways to express it that won't hurt you or
other people. More about this later on in the book.

3

BARGAINING

If I do the housework I won't have to make that call.

If I go to church all year God will make things all right.

You may bargain with your friends and family.

Or your bargains may be with God (or whatever all-powerful force you believe in).

Bargaining can be a way of trying to control change or put off the inevitable.

4

SADNESS & DEPRESSION

My life is meaningless.

What's the point?

I don't feel like doing anything.

If only I'd known.

If only it could be the way it was …

Crisis is about something ending. At some point it sinks in that life will never be quite the same again.

You begin to feel sad and grieve for what you have lost.

Your sadness may turn into depression.

You may have very little energy.

And feel low physically, mentally, emotionally and spiritually.

Like night following day,
this is all part of the process.
You won't feel the same for ever.

ACCEPTANCE

5

I've GOT it.

I feel good again.   YES!

At last you start to see things very differently.

Something clicks into place.

Even if nothing has changed on the outside,
you feel different inside.

This stage may seem a long way off,
but you have the power to get there.

Acceptance is not defeat.
When we accept reality, we become winners.

Going with the flow

What you feel in each stage of the crisis
is important, no matter how hard it is.
The only way out is through.
Give yourself permission to see the crisis as

a fluid

process

always moving and changing.
You will definitely not stay where you are now, for ever.

TRUST THE PROCESS

Your instinct may be to fight the crisis.
I WON'T give up.

Accepting change may seem like accepting defeat.
I WON'T give in.

With all the courage and energy you have,
you try to force life back into its old pattern.
I HAVE to fix things somehow.

The truth is that
you can't control the crisis.
Give yourself permission to stop fighting and

go with the flow

It can feel very liberating, and a huge relief.

Think of your crisis like a knot in a rope. Pull the ends of the rope, and the knot tightens. Push the ends in towards the knot, and it starts to loosen. Resisting the crisis is like pulling the ends of the knot. When you go with the flow, you help the knot loosen.

Or think of your crisis as a current taking you out to sea. When you fight the current, all you do is tire yourself out. It's stronger than you are. Go with the flow until the current sets you free.

Allow yourself to stop resisting the process.

WHERE YOU ARE IS WHERE YOU NEED TO BE

Feelings

Feelings just are.

They have no logic.

They aren't right or wrong.
They're just there.
If we accept them, they stay for a while

and then move on.

Feelings are like the weather.

Sometimes it rains.

Then the rain stops and the sun comes out.
Now and then there's a thunderstorm,
but that too moves on.

                                    Just like feelings.

Feelings you'd rather not have

anger
guilt
fear
doubt
bitterness
jealousy
shame
hatred
remorse
envy
sadness
resentment
despair
insecurity

You may have been brought up not
to show some feelings.

You may not like to admit, even
to yourself, that you have them.

But in the long run it doesn't help to deny feelings
or pretend they aren't there.

Volcano

Burying feelings deep inside just doesn't work.
It's like trying to plug a volcano that's about to erupt.

THE PRESSURE
GOES ON BUILDING
UNTIL THERE'S
AN EXPLOSION!

Buried feelings pour out
with a force you can't control,
often when you least expect or want it.
Noticing your feelings, including ones
you'd rather not have, is useful here.

NOTICE

how you feel

Noticing means paying attention,
it doesn't mean judging.
Noticing brings into consciousness
what was previously unconscious.

There's a lot going on

you

inside

The more you notice,
the more choices you give yourself.

The more you notice, the more you find
out what you're really like.

Who are you?

As we grow up, we learn to
edit parts of ourselves that
we think are unacceptable or
unlovable to the people around us.
We want to fit in so we cut these
'unacceptable' parts out of the
version of ourselves that
we show the world.

We may even end up believing
we ARE the edited version.

anger
competitiveness
fear
jealousy
sexual feelings
self-doubt

I don't tell lies.
I'm never jealous.
I mustn't cry.
I mustn't make mistakes.

As life goes on, these parts of ourselves
that we'd prefer to deny have a nasty way
of demanding attention. Pretending they
don't exist is hard work.
I must stay in control.

We can't relax and go with life's flow
if we have to watch ourselves all the
time to check the 'unacceptable' parts
aren't showing.
Do I look upset?

Only when we accept ALL our parts –
whether we like them or not – can we experience
life fully. Just like the seasons of the year, we need
the icy cold of winter and the scorching heat of
summer. From one extreme to the other, and
all the temperatures in between.

We need them all.

If we don't allow
ourselves to
feel sad, we cut
ourselves off
from joy.

Accepting all of yourself

Accepting all your feelings may feel uncomfortable at first. But the parts you're reclaiming are not *all* of you. Remember there is more of you, even though sometimes it won't feel like that.

Allow yourself to

change and

grow

however uncomfortable it feels.

LET YOUR THOUGHTS
AND FEELINGS BE PRESENT

They will soon move on.

Distractions

You may spend a lot of time trying to
distract yourself, especially at first. You may:

act bright and breezy,
cracking jokes when
inside you feel
like crying

immerse yourself
in things that have
nothing to do with
the crisis, like stories
in the newspapers
or world events

spend all your
time trying to solve
other people's
problems

turn into a couch potato who watches TV day and night

do nothing but work, or nothing but play

distract yourself with addictions: drink, drugs, cigarettes, sex, caffeine, sleeping pills, anti-depressants, tranquillizers

We are experts at finding ways to distract ourselves.

Notice your distractions

Try to notice the ways you distract yourself.
They're a natural part of the process.

There is a time for everything.
A time to distract and deny,
a time to notice and acknowledge.

Where are you in this cycle?

Wherever you are,
you won't stay
in the same place
for ever.

When it's time to stop

Over time, distractions create a kind of deadness.

Trying to shut out the crisis or take your
mind off it uses huge amounts of energy.
It becomes exhausting.

It can create its own problems and more pain
than the crisis itself.

Notice what you're doing.
Ask yourself what you're getting
from the distractions you're using.
What's your payoff?

When you are ready, something will shift inside
you, and you will be strong enough to move on.

Trust the process!

alone

You may feel you can't bear to be with anyone,
even people who are trying to help.
You're like a wounded animal
who
wants
to
hide somewhere
dark

If that's how you feel, OK.
It's part of the process of change,
and it won't last for ever.
But remember,
you need support too.

Don't cut yourself off too long.

Once you've shut people out, it's hard to let them into your life again.

Notice what's going on inside you.
* How do you feel when you're with people?
* What do you say to them?
* What are the ways you use to shut them out?
* What do you gain by it?
* What's going on in your body?

You could write down your answers in a journal, or express them as drawings – whatever feels right for you.

You don't have to try to change how you feel:
just notice.

You may want to be alone because you don't feel good about yourself. This is a very common part of being in crisis.

It's all my fault.

I'm so sorry for all the pain I'm causing.

I should have stopped it happening.

They don't like me.

Be aware of your feelings.

REMIND YOURSELF
THAT THESE ARE
JUST FEELINGS
INSIDE YOU. WHAT
YOU FEAR ISN'T
NECESSARILY REAL.

The inner critic

We all carry a voice around with us that
whispers in our ear:
You're not good enough.

When something goes wrong, the
whispering gets louder.
You don't deserve to be happy.

We start to feel the voice may be right,
that we don't deserve to be loved or valued.

This is just not true.

we all deserve
to be loved

You DO deserve to be happy

When your inner critic starts whispering,
notice what's happening, and tell it to buzz off.
Then get to work balancing negative
messages with positive ones.

*I am growing and learning
every day.*

I love, respect and honour myself.

I have the power to heal myself.

Be positive about yourself

Say these messages to yourself morning and night.
Repeat them looking at yourself in the mirror.
Write them out every day in a journal, or on cards
to stick up where you'll see them a lot.

You may feel embarrassed or strange at first.
Keep trying and you'll get used to it.
The more positive messages, the better.
Negative messages are very strong.

IT TAKES TIME AND PRACTICE TO REDRESS THE BALANCE

Celebrate yourself

Here are some more positive messages to try:

I take in new knowledge and information easily and joyfully

I am open to living and knowing my true self

I grow and prosper through performing my life's work

I value myself

I am rich and prosperous in every way

I trust myself to learn what I need to

I love expressing who I am in creative ways

I am loved and supported by family and friends

I accept myself exactly as I am

I am able to ask for support when I need it

I am allowed to make mistakes

You matter

Give yourself some of the things you love
and enjoy whenever you can:

take a
long
bath

go for a walk
outside, some
place beautiful

listen to
music you
love

read
self-help
books

use
essential
oils

spend time with
young children
or animals

treat yourself
to a meal out

light a
candle

cover your
walls with
inspiring
pictures

be kind
to yourself

Accept nature's help

Get out into nature as often as you can.
Its beauty will nourish you and feed your soul.
Open your eyes to the colours of leaves and flowers.

them *in*

Climb a hill and see the bigger picture.
See how the landscape changes
with the changing seasons.
Take photographs, draw,
collect leaves, stones or cones.

We are all part of the
natural world and
nature helps us heal
body, mind and soul.

One day you will wake up and it will
be Spring in your inner world too.
You will feel lighter and easier.
The pain will have moved on.
Trust the process.

Fear

Change brings up fear of the unknown.
We keep asking ourselves: what if ...?
Step back from your fear by noticing it.

What does fear feel like physically?
Your body may know you're afraid
before your mind does.

I feel sick.

I'm shaky.

How does fear affect the way
you function mentally?

I can't concentrate.

I can't forget about it.

How does it affect your ordinary life?

I can't go out.

I can't talk to anyone.

You feel afraid,
but your fear is not all of you.
Try to let go of WHAT IF
and stay with WHAT IS.

You are not alone

Crisis is a part of life and everyone goes through it.

bank managers

teachers

bus drivers

doctors

accountants

everyone

supermarket cashiers

tax inspectors

politicians

people you pass on the street

lawyers

Remind yourself that crisis can bring
change, growth, beauty, transformation.

You don't have to hang on to old patterns.
You don't have to distract, resist, deny.
There is another way: let the pain of crisis into
your being, knowing it won't drown you.
The pain is a part of you, not all of you.

There's no quick fix

It's hard to accept the pain of crisis.
We long to fix it – make it better.
We find ourselves grabbing at anything –
a new relationship, a new house, a new job,
a holiday – to make the pain go away.

A quick fix may feel good for a while
but it's not the same as a real solution.
Solutions generally take time. You can't rush them.

Try, if you can, to have patience.
The pain will move on of its own accord
when the time is right – not necessarily
when you want it to.

trust the process

ANGER

I feel like screaming.   I want to hit someone.

I feel hot all over.

Anger can be an overwhelming experience.
It can feel as if it blots out everything else.
Noticing how you feel can help.

Notice how your body reacts
and what you think when you're angry.

Noticing is like taking a step away from the anger.
The more you do this, the better you will get at it.

Your anger is only **1** part
of you.

You have anger but you are not only anger.

DANGER!
BURIED
ANGER

Many of us bury our anger

D
E
E
P

INSIDE

We don't know what else to do with it.

Buried anger is

It's out of reach, where we can't express it
or resolve it. It stays there inside us, affecting
the choices we make without our being aware
of it. It can make us ill in all sorts of ways.

There are far better ways to cope with anger
in a safe, non-violent, direct way.

Safe ways to use anger

Use your anger to give you the energy to:

Be creative with your anger:

beat a drum

write
about it

splash
out with
paints

decorate
a room

draw

ANGER CAN BE CONSTRUCTIVE, AUTHENTIC AND VITAL
How do you express your anger?
How would you like to express it?

Emotional hygiene

Take care of your emotions daily,
as regularly as you care for your teeth.
Twice a day, morning and evening,
HIT THE MATTRESS WITH A TENNIS RACKET.

Hold the racket with both hands
and swing it down on the bed.
Express what you're feeling in words or sounds:

AAARRGGGHH!

I hate you!

CAUTION: Best do this when you are alone, or people will wonder what all the noise is about. And make sure the bed's empty before you start ...

Blaming

Sometimes we want to blame other people
for the pain we are feeling.
It's her fault: she told me to do it.

If only other people hadn't behaved so badly
the crisis would never have happened.
I was right, you were wrong.

It may feel safe to blame other people
for the crisis, but blaming keeps you stuck.
It makes you a victim.

Would you
rather be
RIGHT
OR HAPPY ?
It's your choice.

Don't be a victim

The way not to be a victim is to

TAKE BACK INTO YOUR OWN LIFE POWER, RESPONSIBILITY AND CHOICE.

When others give you advice,
make up your own mind whether
or not to take it. It's up to you.

Be aware of your choices.
A victim is a puppet. When someone
pulls their strings they move automatically.

NOTICE IF THIS HAPPENS TO YOU

and start pulling your own strings.

IS FOR RESPONSIBILITY

When we take responsibility for our lives,
we sometimes get it wrong.
We are all imperfect human beings.
We make mistakes.

M

IS FOR MISTAKES

Don't be hard on yourself if you don't get things
right the first time, or the second or third.
Mistakes are how we learn and grow.
Everyone is allowed to make mistakes,
including you.

control

We like to fool ourselves that we are in control
of our lives, but how much control do we have?

We can't control what other people think,
or feel or do. We can't control natural disasters,
or world events like war or recession.
Changes we can't control go on around us
and inside us every day.

Ultimately our control is an illusion.

Serenity

Trying to control the uncontrollable
is a short-cut to stress and exhaustion.
Fighting a battle we can't win
makes us feel less safe, not more.

When we
truly go with
the flow of life,
we allow ourselves
to grow and
FEEL SAFE.

Support

In a crisis, it is important to find good support.
No one has to go it alone.
You need people to support you:
who don't judge you
who'll listen to you
who don't try to censor you
who treat what you say as confidential.

IN CRISIS YOU NEED
A SAFE SPACE

It's important to support yourself too.
Be kind to yourself.
Eat sensibly.
Get as much rest as you can.

And say no to advice and suggestions
that don't feel right for you.

Getting outside support

You could get support from

A SUPPORT GROUP

YOUR DOCTOR

A COUNSELLOR

YOUR FRIENDS YOUR FAMILY

or from a mixture of them all.

You may feel worse after spending time with
some people.

These may include people who:
tell you what you ought to do or feel
repeat what you've said to other people
want to do all the talking
tell you you're mad
criticize you.

TRUST YOUR GUT FEELINGS

Communicate

People aren't mind readers.
They can only give you what you want,
if you tell them clearly what that is.
The clearer you are, the more chance
you have of getting the support you need.
What kind of support could you use right now?
Try making a list.

If you don't know what you want yet, it's OK.
Be patient. You'll soon become an expert.

Could you babysit for me tomorrow?

Would you go to see the lawyer with me?

I want someone to listen.

I'd like to talk about it.

Can we take it in turns?

I need time alone.

I'd like us to spend more time together.

Will you help me with this letter?

I'd like you to come with me tonight.

Will you cook at the weekend?

All I need is a hug.

Doing ...

children home work friends parents community

We spend a lot of time DOING,
running from place to place,
juggling all the things
in our lives.

... and being

Be sure that you make time just to

be

Do some **soul work.**
Set aside time each day for doing
something that lifts your heart.

You don't have to go to a special place
to do soul work. It happens within you,
and you can do it anywhere:
listening to music, gazing at the sunset,
taking a walk ...
whatever makes your heart sing.

This is just one kind of soul work.

Sit in a comfortable chair, turn off the
phone and just be with yourself.

Concentrate on your breath.
You don't have to change it,
just notice it and allow it to be.

Check whether you are holding
any tension in your body.
Noticing where the tension is
may be enough to shift it.

Allow whatever thoughts, feelings
or body sensations you have
to be present. Don't get caught up
in any particular one.
Stay an observer. Notice them
and let them move on.

Connect with a quiet place within you
and stay there for as long as you need.
This place is always there. You can make
a return visit whenever you like.

make
space

in your life for being creativ
Creating is a way to discover more about yoursel

You matter

Maybe you're creative without acknowledging it: a cook or a gardener? Experiment with different ways of being creative. Choose one that feels right for you.

Being creative is not about producing works of art, it's about finding ways to express what is going on inside you. You may be surprised what you can learn about yourself this way.

You needn't show your work to anyone.
If you have not worked this way before,
be patient with yourself. It may take a while
before you allow your creativity to flow.
The more you do it, the more you are able to do it.

ACCEPTANCE

To accept is to free yourself from old, outdated ways of being, ways that no longer serve you.

acceptance gives you

POWER

It allows you to see the whole picture.
It's the goal you were aiming for all along.

I accept myself.
I accept other people.
I accept what's happened.

Acceptance is the last stage of the process of crisis.

However, these stages last for different lengths of time and sometimes exist side by side.

You may accept some changes sooner than others, letting go of old beliefs one by one to make room for new ones.

The more you accept, the easier it is to move on.

Your process may not be quite over yet.

KEEP TRUSTING THE PROCESS!

Your wish list for a new life

What would you like more of in your life?

love ★ *harmonious relationships* ★ *wisdom*

Write a list of whatever it is you want.

understanding ★ *fun* ★ *self-esteem* ★ *integrity*

In what ways would your life change
if you got your wish?

safety ★ *peace* ★ *fulfilment* ★ *honesty* ★ *trust*

How would you know without a doubt
that you'd got there?

passion ★ *laughter* ★ *feeling* ★ *openness* ★ *forgiveness*

For each item on your wish list, close your eyes and allow an image to present itself to you. Visualize the image as clearly as you can. When you've finished, put the list away. Visualize your chosen images often, reminding yourself of all they mean to you. Do this for at least 3 months, then take out the list again: Is your life opening up to make room for the qualities and experiences you are looking for?

Believe and all things are possible.

The hidden gift

Every crisis has a gift for us.
This gift will not be obvious immediately,
but it will be there nevertheless.
Remind yourself about it from time to time.

What will this gift be?

- ★ *a more authentic way of living*
- ★ *more of a sense of self*
- ★ *feeling bigger inside, as if there is more of you*
- ★ *more choice and clarity*
- ★ *an appreciation of everyday life*

Each gift is unique and individual
and can't be predicted.
You will recognize it when it is there!

what is your

gift?

HELPING YOURSELF THROUGH A CRISIS: THE BASICS

★ **GET GOOD SUPPORT.** If it's hard to talk freely to friends or family, try a doctor, counsellor or one of the organizations listed on pages 127-8. Good support helps. No one has to go it alone.

★ **EAT WHAT YOU CAN.** Food may be the last thing you feel like, but your body will cope better with the stress of crisis if you don't starve yourself. You are worth feeding properly.

★ **TRY TO REST.** If you can't sleep, even lying down does some good. You could try your doctor or complementary remedies if lack of sleep really troubles you.

★ **TRY GENTLE EXERCISE** if you have the energy: a walk outside in natural surroundings may help you relax, give you an appetite, and encourage you to sleep.

★ **TRY ANTI-STRESS TECHNIQUES** such as meditation and deep, slow breathing to help you through stressful periods. These techniques are likely to help more than escaping from your troubles into drink, drugs and other distractions.

★ **TUNE IN TO YOURSELF.** It's easier to cope with a crisis effectively when you're aware of what is going on inside you – body, mind and feelings.

★ **GO WITH THE FLOW.** No matter what you do, the crisis will go on until it reaches its natural ending. It's less painful and exhausting to accept the process than to pour all your energy into resisting it.

★ **WORK ON YOUR SELF-ESTEEM.** Balance your inner critic's negative messages with positive ones. List your own good qualities. Be as kind to yourself as you can. Focusing on guilt, self-criticism and self-blame doesn't help you find a way through the crisis.

★ **AVOID BLAMING OTHER PEOPLE.** Blaming keeps you stuck in the role of victim. Concentrate instead on what you can do to improve your own situation.

★ **CHOOSE HOPE.** The pain of crisis doesn't have to last for ever. Choosing to look forward to a time when you will feel good about life again is one of the most helpful – and realistic – things you can do.

HELPING SOMEONE ELSE IN CRISIS

★ **LISTEN.** Give your undivided attention even if they sometimes repeat themselves or are hard to follow. Listening may not seem like much, but it's often the most important help you can give.

★ **ALLOW THEM TO EXPRESS THEIR FEELINGS** whatever these may be. Don't try to cheer them up, or tell them not to be sad or angry. Strong feelings are natural in crisis. The more they express them, the quicker the healing process.

★ **DON'T JUDGE.** Their inner critic will be working overtime. Negative messages and criticism (like 'I told you so,' or 'It's a shame you said that') are the last thing they need right now.

★ **NEVER SAY SHOULD, OUGHT OR MUST.** It's their crisis and their responsibility to make judgements and decisions — when they are ready to do so.

★ **DON'T TELL THEM WHAT TO DO.** Advice that seems obvious to you may strike them as way off course. It's OK to make a suggestion, but be prepared to let it drop, even if you're quite sure you're right.

★ **TRUST THE PROCESS** and encourage them to do the same. Mirror back their feelings and thoughts every now and then, repeating back what they have just said. If they say 'I lost control,' you can say 'You feel you lost control'? Things can sound different when we hear someone else voice them.

★ **REMIND THEM** that what they are feeling is only part of them, even though it may feel as if it's all of them.

★ **TELL THEM YOU CARE ABOUT/LOVE THEM** even if you think they already know that.

★ **BE REALISTIC ABOUT THE SUPPORT YOU CAN GIVE.** You may feel that you'll stand by them through thick and thin, but take care not to offer more than you can reliably deliver.

★ Last but not least ... **BE KIND TO YOURSELF.** Supporting someone else through a crisis can leave you feeling drained. Notice what's going on inside you, and take time off to relax and recover, whenever you need to.

ABOUT SALLY-ANN LIPSON

In 1989 I was a theatrical agent but wanted to change
direction. I stopped work and gave myself a couple of
months to re-think my career. Looking back, I can see
I was unconsciously giving myself space to unpack my
unwanted baggage: the sort of stuff we all accumulate
through life. The outside structure of my life had
changed dramatically over the previous few years, and
slowly – and incredibly uncomfortably – my inner world
had changed too. I felt insecure and vulnerable.

I was working part time for a dear friend and also crying
on her shoulder. After what seemed like many hours of
listening to me, she suggested I go and see a
Psychosynthesis counsellor, and gave me a name and
number. I remember feeling nervous and frustrated
about our initial meeting. There was so much I wanted to
talk about, I felt full up. On the other hand, quite rightly,
she concentrated on getting a personal history from me.
However, from there on in, what a relief! I started to learn
to unload my overwhelming thoughts and feelings, and
began to realize that although I felt vulnerable, these
feelings were not all I was about. At first it was just words,
but I gradually started to grow – from the inside.

I found Psychosynthesis fascinating. It seemed to complement the process I was going through. It felt like coming home, bringing more choice and balance into my life, enriching me as a person. I am fascinated by human behaviour and eventually my counsellor encouraged me to take a short course on Psychosynthesis. One thing led to another and eventually I found myself undertaking professional training. I qualified in 1996 and now run a private practice in North London.

If every crisis has a gift for us, then mine was discovering Psychosynthesis, which has given me the tools to bring more depth, purpose and joy into my life.

The process of writing this book has been cathartic, and has psychologically helped me through a crisis. I want to thank Kathryn Cave for giving me the original idea, for her vision, patience and creativity; my support team for all the time, encouragement and wisdom they have given me; my children, stepchildren and grandchildren for their love and inspiration; and special thanks to Robert, my husband – he is the wind beneath my wings.

USEFUL CONTACT DETAILS

Alcoholics Anonymous (adults)
& **Alateen** (for young people aged
12-20 who have been affected by
someone else's drinking)
01904 644026

Al-Anon
(support for families and
friends of problem drinkers)
020 7403 0888

**British Association of
Counsellors**
(information line) 01788 578328

Cancer Resource Centre
0171 924 3924

Childline
(helpline for children 18 and under)
0800 1111

Cruise
(bereavement helpline)
0181 332 7227

Eating Disorders Association
01603 621 414
or 01603 765 050
(for callers18 and under)

Gamblers Anonymous
(and **Gam-Anon** for relatives
of gamblers) 0171 384 3040

Gingerbread
(provides lone parents with
support & advice)
0800 0184318

MIND
(mental health helpline)
0345 660163

Narcotics Anonymous
0171 730 0009

National Debtline
(provides expert advice and a self-help
information pack free of charge)
0645 500 511

Parentline
(support for parents or carers)
0808 800222

**The Psychosynthesis &
Education Trust**
0171 403 2100

Relate
(relationship guidance)
01788 573241

The Samaritans
0345 909090

Saneline
(mental health helpline
for carers, sufferers or friends)
0345 678000

Smokers Quitline
0800 002200

Survivors of Incest Anonymous
(for women)
0171 831 6946

Survivors
(Help for male survivors of
incest/sexual abuse)
0171 833 3737

Victim Supportline
(practical and emotional support
for victims and witnesses of crime)
0845 303 0900

**Women's Aid National
Domestic Violence Helpline**
0345 023468